Card Tricks for Beginners

Easy Card Magic Tricks for Aspiring Magicians to Amaze Their Crowd

Andrew West

Table of Contents

Introduction

Welcome magicians! Or at least those who hope to become magicians, in which case, welcome hopefuls! Card magic, compared to other forms of trickery, is relatively new, they've only been around for at least a couple thousand years, but personally I find them the most fun to watch and the most fun to perform.

However, it can be a little hard to get started on actually performing card tricks of your own, you can watch them yet find yourself falling a little flat on the excitement when it comes to trying to copy them on your own, especially if you don't know exactly how the tricks are actually done. But that is what I am here to do with you, to teach some amazing beginner tricks for the aspiring magician.

Whether you are a kid who just wants to learn how to impress your family and friends, or an adult who wants to walk the path of stage magic, this book is here to help make it easy for you to learn and understand some beginner's card tricks that will be sure to amaze your audience.

How This Book Will Work

To help make things easier for you, I will begin by explaining some very basics about card tricks, such as the makeup of a deck, skills with their definitions and some friendly advice before we move onto the tricks themselves. But I won't just be throwing a list of tricks at you, instead I will be breaking down the tricks into star ratings that determine if they are a very basic beginner trick (one star) to "advanced" beginner tricks (five stars), which is to help you along your path to mastery.

Now let's make some magic!

CHAPTER ONE:

Card Deck Basics

If you are a true beginner and have never even played a game with a deck of cards before and are a little lost on the details about what is in a card deck, then this is the chapter for you; if you are familiar with the basic card deck then you are free to skip onto the next chapter.

First of all, card decks, the ones either used for games or for tricks like the kind in this book, have a standard when it comes to how they are set up; meaning that they will be exactly the same, all of them. A "standard" card deck will have the following attributes:

- The total number of cards in a deck is fifty-two, which is certainly a lot when you think about it even if you don't have trouble with holding an entirely full deck in your hands.

- For these fifty-two cards, they are divided into thirteen "ranks" and there are two categories of ranks that vary depending on the situation. But for both ranks, they include the numbers two through ten, jack, queen, king and ace.

- One category is called "Ace High" which refers to when an ace outranks the king, the other category is "Ace Low" which in when an ace is outranked by the two; but there will be some situations where an ace can be both high and low, it all depends on the situational rules.

- What these fifty-two cards are also divided into are "suits", of which there are four: clubs, diamonds, hearts and spades. Each suit contains one of each card rank, so there are thirteen clubs, thirteen diamonds, thirteen hearts and thirteen spades.

- Furthermore these four suits come in only two colors, black and red. There are two suits per color, with clubs and spades being black and diamonds and hearts being red, which makes up a total of twenty-six cards of each color.

- Going back to the "ranks", this means that each rank holds four cards, one of each suit.

- The three cards that are known as the jacks, queens and kings are referred to as "face cards"; there are a dozen face cards per deck, with three or one of each of the three per suit and four of each per rank.

- Decks also typically come with "joker" cards, but whether or not it is even used is also dependent on the situation the decks are being used in.

- All wrapped up nice and neatly right? Now let us move onto the development and understanding of the basics of card tricks themselves.

CHAPTER TWO:

Card Trick Skill Basics

For this chapter I will be briefly discussing the basic skills that are needed in order to perform the card tricks listed in this book; some of them are used in a lot of tricks while some of them are used in only a few of them and some tricks may even need more than one to make them work!

- **Card counting:** As the name implies, you are counting the cards, making sure that you have picked up or laid out the right number of cards and if they are in the right order. There are a few ways to do this, but the typical way to do this is to assign "values" to each card and have a tally sheet in your head where you start at zero and count with each card chosen; such as a positive one for number cards or a negative one for face cards or some other combination that is easy for you to remember.

- **Card cutting:** All but the most basic of beginner's are likely to know that "cutting the cards" doesn't actually mean cutting up the cards with a sharp object, in the case of magic and games it refers to the division of the deck in certain ways by taking a pile off the top of the deck. While they won't be covered here, there are ways out there where you can impress people by cutting a deck with fancy one handed tricks if you practice enough.

- **Card Forcing:** is a tricky skill to master, as the goal is to make your volunteer pick the card you want while making it seem like they had a choice in choosing a random card; there are roughly a couple of ways of doing this. As hard as this skill is to master, there is an advantage of using this skill to make up your own card tricks once you have mastered it!

- **Card peeking:** This means you are taking a secret look at a certain card where you are memorizing the suit and number of the card without your audience realizing that you are even doing it; this is in fact one of the more popular tricks used out there. Depending on the trick, there are a few ways to do it, such as holding the deck face down with one hand with the thumb on the nearest short side and the rest of the fingers on the farthest and making it where you a tapping a long side on a nearby table and taking the opportunity to look at the bottom card.

- **Memory:** If you want to eventually become a master at card tricks, you have to have a good memory, even if you are just a beginner who is reading this book for that reason. It is especially important in the cases where you are attempting a trick that has several stages that will only be successful if you remember them clearly and in the right order.

- **Misdirection**: In order for tricks to work, you need to keep the audience from figuring out what you are really doing, a good way to do this is to do things that have nothing to do with the trick in question to keep your audience distracted enough from watching your every move.

- **Observation:** Like with your memory, you need to have good observational skills when pulling off a good trick, you need to be aware of what is going on around you at all times.

- **Props:** Occasionally props are needed when performing a successful card trick and they will vary from trick to trick; in this book each will be noted as required for a certain trick.

- **Sleight of hand:** This is basically just an umbrella term that refers to being able to secretly move things around with your hands in a way that the audience is under the impression that you are doing something else, it differs from misdirection in that sleight of hand is moving your hands rather than simply providing a distraction like the former. Here are a few examples of sleight of hand tricks that you might come across in this book,

- **Double Lift:** Double lifting cards is when you are picking up two cards in a way that is supposed to make it look like you are only picking up one by showing the audience the second card you've picked up rather than the top one that you are keeping a secret. Unlike other skills, there is really only one way to perform a Double Lift skill as detailed below:

  - Hold the deck in your left hand facing down

  - Use your right hand by putting the thumb on the back of the top card and your fingers on the far end to search for the first two top cards

  - As you lift up the cards, press them slightly so that they bend just a little bit, the cards should stick together and it should look to the audience that you only picked up only a single card.

- **False Cut:** This refers to fooling your audience into thinking that you are cutting the deck in a fair way, but the reality of it is that you are keeping the deck in the same order or that you're keeping one or more cards at the bottom of the deck.

- **False Shuffle:** This means fooling the audience into thinking that you are in fact mixing up cards when in actuality, you are controlling the deck. This skill is useful if you are wanting to keep a card or a group of cards on the top or bottom of the deck. There are several ways of doing this, so practice is essential in finding which one is a good fit for a certain trick.

- **Spelling:** As weird as this might sound, some tricks actually need to have a word spelled out in order for it to work. To do this successfully, you have to learn how to spell the word and practice spelling it if needed, before you perform the trick to keep from making mistakes.

- **Stacking the deck:** This means for you to secretly arrange the cards in one or more ways so some of them are in a certain order that only the magician knows but the audience doesn't; it's typically done before a trick is performed and of course needs that good memory if you want to be successful in remembering which card is where.

CHAPTER THREE:

One Star Tricks

Abracadabra

Skills Needed

- Card Counting
- Spelling

Steps

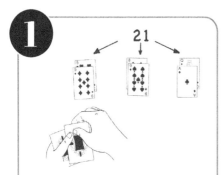

Deal twenty-one cards into three columns with seven cards in each column and lay them all face up in an up to down order.

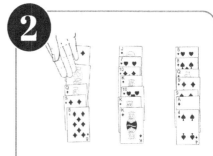

Have a volunteer pick one of the cards, but they aren't supposed to tell you which one, what they are supposed to tell you is which of the three columns it is in.

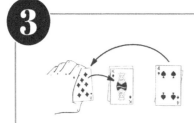

Pick up the three columns, but make sure that you pick up the cards in the same order that you put them down; however, the column that was picked by the volunteer should be picked up second, so that it is sandwiched between the other two columns.

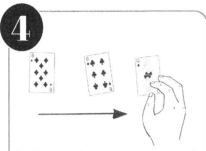

4 Deal out the twenty-one cards again, but instead of dealing them up to down, lay them out left to right and ask your volunteer which column it is in now.

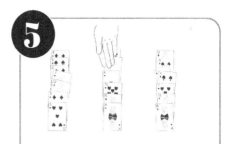

5 Now repeat step three while still making sure that the cards are still in order and that the column containing the volunteer's chosen card is again in between the other two.

6

A-B-R-A-C-A-
D-A-B-R-A

11

Deal the cards into a pile face down while spelling out "abracadabra", saying one letter for each card that you are putting down. When you get to the ending "a", hold the corresponding card in your hand and ask the volunteer their chosen card's name and if you did all of this right, their chosen card should be revealed when you reveal it.

Back Palm Vanish
(Single Card)

Skills Needed

- Misdirection
- Sleight of Hand

Steps

1 Hold the card on the bottom between your thumb and middle finger, a quarter inch from the bottom and tight, but not tight enough where it can't move.

2 Wave the card around to fool the audience by loosening your grip and using your ring finger to move the card.

3 Wrap your index and pinky around the card's edges as you're waving, be careful not to move your thumb.

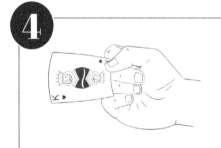

4 Use your index and pinky to curve the card and tuck your middle and ring beneath the edge by lining up the fingernails of the latter two fingers with the edge.

5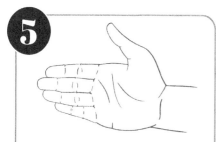

Extend all fingers to open your hand, the card will then move to the back of your hand as the index and pinky hold it, but keep them squeezed together to keep the audience from seeing the card.

6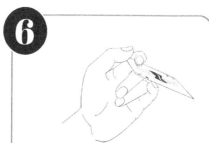

To bring the card back to the front, keep the card between your index and pinky and curl your middle and ring inward, then catch it with your thumb and index so it's back where it was. Don't forget, every movement you make has to be very fast!

* *Note: This is the trick done with only one card, see "Back Palm Vanish (Multiple Cards)" in the next chapter for the trick done with multiple cards.*

Cutting the Four Aces

Skills Needed

- False Cut (optional)
- Stacking the Deck

Preparation

Before you have an audience, take all four of the aces in the deck and put them on top; your volunteer will be the one handling the cards, but they are not in on the trick, so you are the only one who is supposed to know about the deck stacking! You also have the option of performing a false cut before the trick actually begins, it is only optional, but it helps to fool the people around you about the cards being in a random order.

Steps

Ask your volunteer to cut the deck so that they are divided up into four piles that are somewhat equal in number, you need to pay attention to where the four aces ended up.

Point to one of the piles that don't have the aces and have the volunteer pick it up and hold it, then ask them to take three cards off the top and put them at the bottom of the pile.

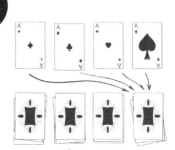

You do have the option to make this easier for you by asking the volunteer to separate the deck by dropping the bottom cards to make the four piles; this would make sure that the aces would end up in a pile that is either to the very left or the very right, which make the next steps make more sense. For this example they will be on the far right and if they ended up in a different pile then you will have to adjust the next steps.

4

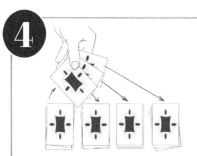

Now ask the volunteer a card from the pile that they are holding into each of the other three piles.

5

Repeat steps three and four with another pile that doesn't have the ace and then repeat again with the last pile that doesn't have an ace.

6

Before we get to the final steps, let us recap that the three non-ace piles have a mix of random cards, but we aren't interested in those; we are interested in the pile with the aces that have three random cards on top which are followed by the four aces.

7

Now we ask the volunteer to repeat steps three and four. It is from the previous steps that the three random cards on the aces are put to the bottom of the pile and then an ace is dealt onto each of the other three piles!

8

It is now time to ask the volunteer to turn over the top card of each pile and when they are turned over, they should be the aces!

Do As I Do

Skills Needed

- Card Peeking
- Memory

Steps

1

You need two decks of cards, different backs are recommended and no cards should be missing. Have your volunteer choose one and tell them to do as you do by shuffling and cutting their deck at the same time as you.

2

As you finish shuffling, take a very quick look at the bottom card of your deck and remember it.

3

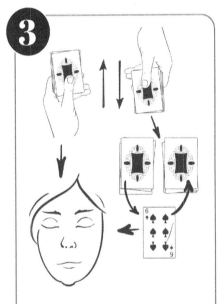

Switch decks with your volunteer and ask them to cut the top half of their deck and put the cards to their right; then have them take the top card of their left pile, remember the card and put it on top of their right pile without showing you.

4

Have them pick up the pile on their left and put them on their right pile, this secretly puts your reference card next to their card, as they are doing, do the same actions, but you don't actually remember your picked card, your reference card is what is important!

5

Switch decks again, then tell your volunteer to look for their card in this deck and pull it out, put it face down. You do the same, except you are looking for your reference card, the card should be to the right and you pull it out and put it face down.

6

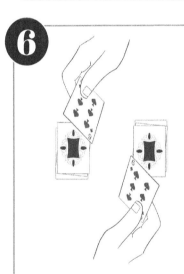

Count to three out loud and flip over both cards, which should be the same!

Power of Four

Skills Needed

- Card Peeking
- Memory
- Misdirection
- Observation

Steps

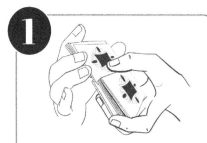

To help sell the magic, have your volunteer be the one to shuffle the deck if they want to.

Now shuffle the deck yourself, but make sure to leave at least the top four cards on the top!

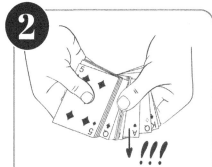

After the shuffling is finished and you receive the deck back, face it up to the both of you and fan them out from the top to the bottom, but while you are doing that, secretly peek at the fourth card from the top as you are spreading them and remember what it is while you are misdirecting by reminding the people listening that the cards are in a random order.

4

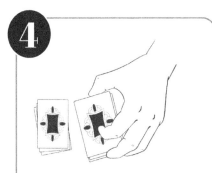

Tell the volunteer to cut the deck in half whatever way they want, but of course you know that the fourth card from the top of the pile that used to be on the deck is the card.

5

You are going to count out four cards from the pile that were from the bottom of the deck while telling your volunteer that the fourth card from this pile will tell you which is the fourth card in the other pile, the one that you already know.

6

Look at this fourth card but do not show the volunteer, instead look at it and memorize this one, and announce that this card tells you that the fourth card in the other pile is the first card.

7

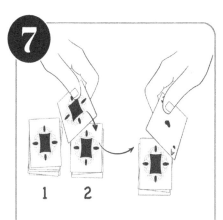

1   2

Put this second memorized card back and count out the four cards from the top of the other pile which should be the first card to the amazement of your audience!

8

But there's more! Repeat step three by shuffling the cards but leaving the second card as the fourth card from the top this time, repeat steps four and five to receive and memorize yet another card and then reveal your true "prediction" and repeat steps three, four and five again and again until you feel ready to move on.

CHAPTER FOUR:

Two Star Tricks

Back Palm Vanish
(Multiple Cards)

Skills Needed

- Misdirection
- Sleight of Hand

Steps

1

First, you need to make yourself comfortable with holding multiple cards in the back palm position (you do it the same way you would a single card) however it puts more tension in your fingers.

2

Make sure that the cards are all lined up with no edges showing.

3

You need to curl your middle and ring fingers to bring the cards forward, but only enough for them to be reachable to your thumb.

Loosen your pinky and put your thumb on the right corner to remove it, extend the index to release the card in front while keeping the rest between the pinky and index.

Open your hand, it will cause the other cards to return to the back palm and out of the audience's view; then drop the card that you had revealed so you can reveal another card.

Repeat the process with the remaining cards until you have revealed all the ones you had. It's best to begin with three cards, but there really isn't a limit to how many you can do this trick with!

Make A Prediction

Skills Needed

- False Cut
- False Shuffle
- Stacking the Deck

Preparation

The deck stacking is a little complicated with this one, first you separate all four of the suits of a single card type, you will also take out a five and three random cards. Arrange it so the five is at the top of the deck, then the three random cards and three of the four that you've picked and then put these seven cards on top of the deck with your last card being put somewhere in the middle.

Steps

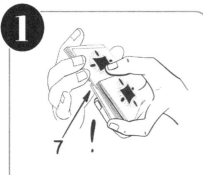

Begin by doing a false shuffle of the deck that keeps the top seven cards on top.

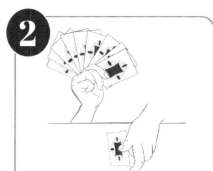

Tell your volunteer that you are going to make a prediction, fan the cards so that they are facing you and find and pick the card you put in the middle, don't let the volunteer see your card, just put it face down on the table.

③

Have the volunteer cut the cards into three equal piles that you will carefully move around if necessary, then put those piles face down and flip over the top card from each and put them in front of the piles, (the five should be in the last pile).

④

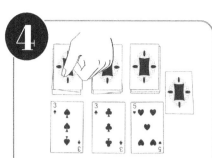

Pick up the first pile and count out the number of cards from the top that matches the card you picked from the top, then put one card on top of the other two piles and set the pile down again.

⑤

Repeat step four with the second pile, and then with the third.

⑥

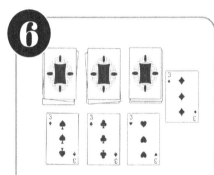

Now turn over your "prediction" card, flip over the top card from the three piles, all four of the cards should be revealed!

Pick a Card

Skills Needed

- Card Peeking
- Memory

Steps

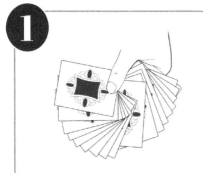

Fan out the cards as you hold them face down, if the audience wants you to shuffle, do so.

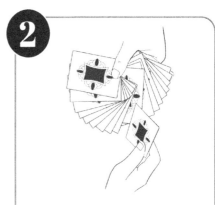

Ask a volunteer to pick any card and pull it out of the deck.

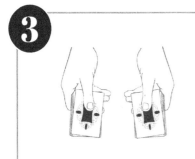

Cut the deck into two stacks after they have pulled their card, with one stack in each hand.

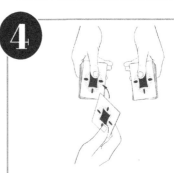

Tell the volunteer to remember the card, and then put it on top of the pile in your left hand.

Quickly look at the bottom card of the right hand pile, you're using it as a reference to find the volunteer's card.

Put the right-hand pile on top of the left hand so the bottom card is next to the volunteer's card.

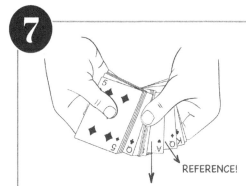

REFERENCE!

Spread the cards on the table face up, try to spy your reference card as fast as you can, it should be on the left hand side of the volunteer's card; but don't be sloppy or you might miss it or take too long looking!

Presto!

Skills Needed

- Card Counting
- Misdirection
- Spelling

Steps

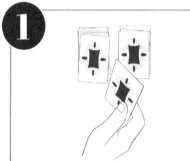

Give to your volunteer a full deck of cards and ask them to deal all of the cards into two piles face down.

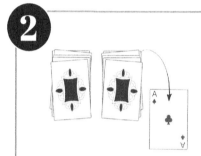

Ask them to look at the bottom card of one of the piles, but not show you their chosen card, and that they have to remember their card.

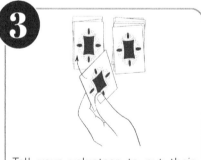

Tell your volunteer to put their chosen pile on top of the other pile and straighten up the deck.

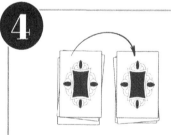

Ask the volunteer to deal the entire deck face down into four piles.

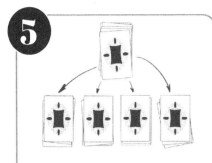

Have them look through each of the piles and tell you which pile has their card.

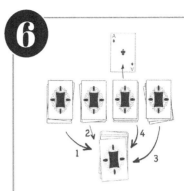

Now you handle the cards, pick them up together to make the deck whole again; but you need to be sure that the pile containing the volunteer's card is placed at the very top. This is where the misdirection comes in as you don't want the audience to know that you have made it easy to identify the card this way.

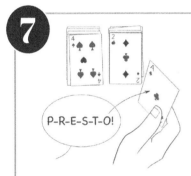

P-R-E-S-T-O!

Give the full deck face down to the volunteer and ask them to deal out the cards face up, they should spell out the word "presto" while doing so, saying one letter for each card that they put down.

Now take the deck from the volunteer and turn over the top card, if this was all completed properly, the top card that you turn over should be the volunteer's chosen card!

The Magic Spell

Skills Needed

- False Shuffle
- Misdirection
- Sleight of Hand
- Spelling

Steps

Ask a volunteer to pick a card from the deck, which is facing down, look at it and memorize it, and then put it back on top of the deck.

Use a false shuffle to make sure that the picked card stays on top of the still face-down deck.

3

Now ask the volunteer the name of the card that they picked and say that you will now reveal it by spelling it out on the table.

4

1   2   3   4

From left to right deal a card face down for each letter you spell out.

5

1   2
3

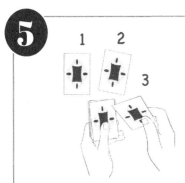

When you get to the last letter, announce that this is the card previously picked (even though you know it isn't) and show it, of course they will say that it isn't their card.

6

Misdirect by pretending to be embarrassed that it didn't work, and then say that you forgot to add some magic!

7

After you talk, pick up the cards off of the table from right to left with one on top of the other and put the pile on top of the deck. Make a gesture with your hand over the deck and give it over to the volunteer.

8

Tell the volunteer that you've added the magic and the trick should work now.

9

Ask them to spell out the name of their card in the same way that you already have done with a card being dealt for each letter, when they are finished, the last card should still be their chosen card!

Upside Down Card

Skills Needed

- Sleight of Hand
- Stacking the Deck

Preparation

This trick involves a minimal "stacking the deck" preparation, you need to turn over the bottom card of the deck so that it is the only card facing up in a deck that is facing down in the beginning.

Steps

Fan the deck out on the table with the cards facing down, but be careful not to expose the face up bottom card and ask your volunteer to pick a card; tell them to memorize it and show everyone else, but don't let you see it.

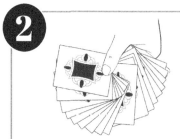

While they are showing off their card to the audience, carefully turn the deck over in your hands so that the deck is facing up in your left hand, except for the top card.

While keeping the deck tight in order to keep the fact that you have reversed the cards a secret, put the volunteer's card face down in the middle of the deck.

4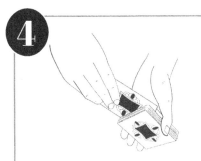

Put the deck behind your back and say that you are going to find the card without looking while secretly turning over the top card so that it is facing up.

5

Take the deck from behind you and fan through it until you find the only face down card and then slowly reveal the selected card.

A-B-R-A-C-A-
D-A-B-R-A

MAKE A DIFFERENCE WITH YOUR REVIEW

Unlock the Power of Generosity

"Money can't buy happiness, but giving it away can." - Freddie Mercury

"Money can't buy happiness, but giving it away can." - Freddie Mercury

People who give without expecting anything back live longer, happier lives. So, if we can try to be like that during our time together, let's do it!

To make that happen, I have a question for you...

Would you help someone you've never met, even if you never got credit for it?

Who is this person, you ask? They are like you. Or, at least, like you used to be. Wanting to learn and needing a little help, but not sure where to look.

Our mission is to make card tricks fun and easy for everyone. Everything I do comes from that mission. And, the only way for me to reach that mission is by connecting with everyone.

This is where you come in. Most people do, in fact, judge a book by its cover (and its reviews). So here's my ask on behalf of a struggling reader you've never met.

Please help that reader by leaving this book a review.

Your gift costs no money and less than 60 seconds to make real, but can change a fellow reader's life forever. Your review could help one more kid amaze their friends, one more beginner feel confident with a deck of cards, one more person discover the joy of magic and one more dream come true.

To get that 'feel good' feeling and help this person for real, all you have to do is leave a review and it takes less than 60 seconds.

Simply scan the QR code below to leave your review:

If you feel good about helping a faceless reader, you are my kind of person. Welcome to the club. You're one of us.

I'm that much more excited to help you learn card tricks easier and more than you can possibly imagine. You'll love the simple tricks I'm about to share in the coming chapters.

Thank you from the bottom of my heart. Now, back to our regularly scheduled programming.

Your biggest fan,

Andrew West

PS - Fun fact: If you provide something of value to another person, it makes you more valuable to them. If you'd like goodwill straight from another reader and you believe this book will help them - send this book their way.

Scan the QR code to leave your review

CHAPTER FIVE:

Three Star Tricks

Eights End Up Together

Skills Needed

- Memory
- Misdirection
- Stacking the Deck

Preparation

Take all eights out from the deck, with the deck face down, put one of them on top of the deck, then put the second one in the tenth position. Turn the deck over and count seven cards and put the last two eights in the eighth and ninth positions.

Steps

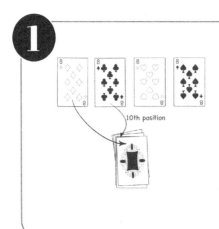

10th position

1 Tell the audience that you are picking a random card and making a prediction. Do this by fanning through once or twice while talking then restacking the deck. Fan them again while inwardly counting to ten, but not looking at the cards, when you get to the tenth card, place your index finger underneath and continue fanning. Pull out that card and put it face down; say that this is your prediction card.

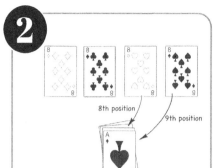

②

8th position

9th position

Turn the deck over and say that you will be counting; pass by the two eights and then tell the audience to say when to stop.

③

Make two piles and put them face down; put the bottom half to the right and the top half on the left.

④

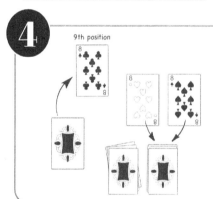

9th position

Turn over the top card on the left pile, which will be the eight you already put there, look and say what it is, and say that it's telling you how many cards to take from the right.

⑤

Count eight cards from the bottom of the right pile while it is still face down and put them into a third pile that is by the one on the left; count out loud for the audience to follow.

⑥

Turn over the top card of the pile you just made, it will be an eight and put it by the first eight. Turn over the pile in your hand to show another eight and put it on the table, then either you or the volunteer will flip over the "prediction" card.

Guess the Bottom Card

Skills Needed

- Card Peeking
- Memory
- Misdirection
- Sleight of Hand

Steps

Hold the deck of cards face down in a hand and do anything that makes the audience believe that the cards are normal.

Take a quick peek at the bottom card before putting them face down and remember it without the audience knowing what you did.

Begin skimming through the cards and ask the audience to stop you when ready. Do this by holding the deck face down and putting the thumb of your other hand underneath the deck and using the first two fingers of the same hand to pull the cards on top a little toward you.

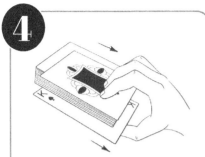

With a single motion, slide the top and bottom cards from the deck, using your index and middle fingers for the former, while using your thumb to take the latter into your hand.

Show the audience the bottom card while holding it away from you and ask them if this is (card name).

Royal Confidante

Skills Needed

- Card Peeking
- False Shuffle
- Memory
- Misdirection
- Sleight of Hand
- Stacking the Deck

Preparation

Not a lot of "stacking the deck" is needed, you just need to put one of the queen's at the bottom of the deck and remember which one you picked.

Steps

①

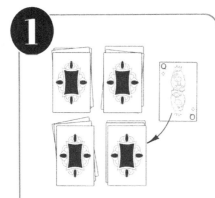

Shuffle the deck, but make sure to keep your queen at the very bottom.

②

Cut the deck into four piles that are all facing down on the table and remember which pile came from the bottom of the deck.

③

Have your volunteer take a card from any of the piles and show it to the audience, but don't show it to you. Then ask them to put it back.

4

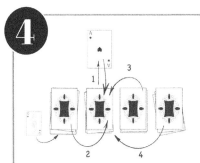

Now put the piles back together as a single deck, but put the bottom pile on top of the picked card; this is to help you know which card was picked as it is now directly under your queen. Then put the other two piles on top of that. If your volunteer had picked the top card of the bottom pile, have them cut the pile again before putting the deck back together, this is to help keep your queen on top of their card.

5

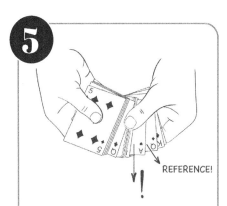

REFERENCE!

Now cut the pack roughly halfway down to make sure that it is away from the chosen card and fan out the cards face up on the table. Look around the cards and say that one of the queens is trying to tell you something.

6

Pick up your chosen queen that is now beneath the volunteer's card because you've turned the pack over; make a show of putting the queen next to your ear and say that she's whispering to you.

7

Now reach for the card that was next to it and say that this is the volunteer's card!

Stop When You Want

Skills Needed

· Sleight of Hand

Preparation

On a piece of paper, write down "the card you will stop at will be-" and the name of your chosen card; put the note loose inside of your wallet and put the chosen card itself in your pocket.

Steps

①

Hand the deck to the volunteer and have them shuffle it; then ask them to deal the cards face down onto the table-make sure they know to deal the cards anywhere and not in a neat pile.

②

While the volunteer is dealing, take out your wallet and keep your chosen card hidden underneath, facing down.

③

Once the volunteer stops dealing, drop your wallet on the top card, adding your card to the pile.

Tell the volunteer to look in your wallet, where they will find and read the note.

Tell them to read the note out loud, then move your wallet and turn over the top card, the one that should be mentioned in your note!

CHAPTER SIX:

Four Star Tricks

Evens and Odds

Skills Needed

- Stacking the Deck

Preparation

For this one you have to "stack the deck" in a way that gives you two piles of cards, one that has even numbers in it and one with odd numbers in it, in the case of face cards, jacks and kings are considered odd and queens are considered even. The result is that the "odd" pile will be slightly bigger than the "evens."

When the two piles are ready, you have to place the pile of "even" cards on top of the "odd" cards, but do not straighten up the deck, keep the "even" pile at a slight enough angle so you can see where the "odd" pile begins but where the audience won't notice.

Steps

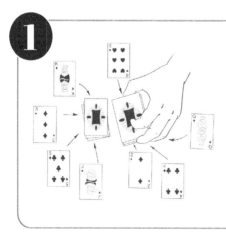

When you have a ready audience, quickly cut the deck into two piles that are facing down, the odd and even cards, but you have to do this as smoothly as possible to keep your audience from figuring out that you had already stacked the deck.

2

Have a volunteer shuffle both piles separately and then pick one, fan out the picked one still facing down and ask the volunteer to pick a card and show it to the audience, but not to you.

3

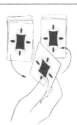

Ask them to put their picked card into the other pile.

4

Have them shuffle this pile as many times as they like.

5

When they are finished, fan through it while it is facing only you and find their card; it won't be difficult since it will be the only one of its kind in the entire pile, whether it's an even in an odd or an odd in an even.

Handkerchief Prediction

Skills Needed

- Card Peeking
- Misdirection
- Sleight of Hand

Props Required

- Handkerchief

Preparation

Look at and memorize the top card of the deck, but not in front of the audience.

Steps

1

Put the deck face down on the table and put the handkerchief over it, your best bet is one that you can't see through

2

Secretly turn the deck face up as you put the handkerchief on while the deck is covered to avoid discovery.

3

Have a volunteer cut the deck while the handkerchief is on it, they will put the top half on the other side of the bottom half, remember which is which and do not shuffle.

Carefully turn the real top half face down again while it is still covered while bringing it out of the handkerchief.

Ask the volunteer to pull the top card from the deck and show the audience, but not you.

Say the cards name and while they are amazed, carefully pull out the rest of the deck while turning it face down.

Magic Elastic

Skills Needed

- Misdirection
- Sleight of Hand

Props Required

- Elastic Band

Steps

Put the elastic band in your pocket before you start the trick. Shuffle the cards and fan them out face down and ask the volunteer to take one.

Ask the volunteer to show your card to the rest of your audience; say that you are turning your back to them as they do this. With your back to the audience you can now do your "sleight of hand" by turning the pack over so that all of the cards are face up; turn over the top card so that it is facing down.

3

Ask the volunteer to hide their card; then turn back to face the audience. Take the elastic band from your pocket and wrap it around the width of the deck.

4

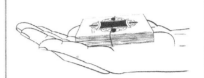

Hold the cards in your left hand with the palm facing up and ask the volunteer to place their card face down into the center of the pack.

5

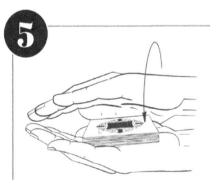

Now you need to do a different "sleight of hand" that you don't want your audience to know what you are doing. Pass the deck from your left hand to your right, while you are doing this, turn your left hand so that the palm is facing downward when it reaches your right.

6

While holding the pack in your right hand, ask the volunteer to twang the band to "make the magic work."

7

Now place the cards back into your left hand but do not turn the deck over and take off the elastic band.

8

Fan the cards out in your hand until you reach your volunteer's card, which should be facing up; but make sure that you don't fan all the way to the bottom, otherwise the audience will see that the bottom card is also facing up!

The Twenty-One Card Trick

Skills Needed

- Memory
- Stacking the Deck (somewhat and optional)

Preparation

This trick requires only twenty-one of the fifty-two cards, you have the option of "deck stacking" beforehand by picking out random cards or...

Steps

1

You can deal them out in front of the audience, the thing to remember is that the number of cards is important, not suits or colors!

2

Fan the cards face down and have a volunteer pick a random card from the pile; they really need to memorize what their card is and show it to the audience, but not to you. Then have them put it back anywhere and shuffle the deck, if the volunteer wants to shuffle, let them.

3

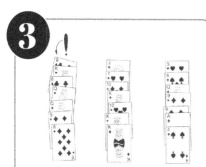

Lay out the cards in a specific way, from left to right, lay out the cards so that they are three cards across with seven cards each, you also have to lay them out across all the way, not laying out one column at a time.

4

Ask the volunteer which column their card is in and they have to be honest, make sure to emphasize that!

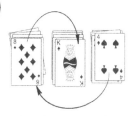

Put each column together as a pile and then stack the pile with their card in it between the other two piles; you have to put the deck back together quick enough that no one notices the particular order!

Repeat steps three to five, do not shuffle the deck in between! Then repeat the process one more time, note that for this last time, because of your deck manipulation, their card will be the fourth card down in their last column pick.

* *Note: This is the basic version of this particular trick, for the more advanced version, see "The Twenty-One Card Trick (Advanced)" in the next chapter.*

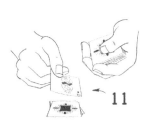

11

After this final deck combining, count out eleven cards and stop at the eleventh card and announce that this is the volunteer's card!

CHAPTER SEVEN

Five Star Tricks

Card Peeking

Skills Needed

- Card Cutting
- Card Peeking
- Misdirection

Steps

Shuffle the deck of cards, but don't forget to take a quick look at the bottom card before straightening them.

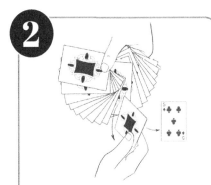

Fan the cards out in your hand facing down and ask the volunteer to pick one and hold onto it; straighten the deck.

3

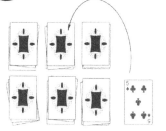

Put the deck face down on the table and tell the volunteer that you are going to cut the cards into small piles which you are going to put on top of each other. Take a small pile off the top of the deck and place it next to the main pile; repeat a few times so you end up with five or six small piles. (Make sure that you make small enough cuts of only a few cards each so you don't run out of cards before the volunteer places their card on top in the next step).

4

Ask the volunteer to place their card on top of one of the piles when they are ready; then pick up the main deck and put it on top of the pile that the volunteer put their card on. The card that you peeked at before will now be on top of the volunteer's card.

5

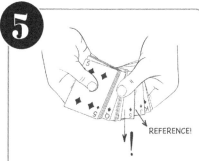

REFERENCE!

Now turn the cards over and fan them out from left to right while making sure that all of the cards can be seen. The volunteer's chosen card should be the one to the right of the one that you had peeked at before!

Forcing the Cards

Skills Needed

- Card Forcing
- False Shuffle
- Stacking the Deck

Props Required

- Envelope
- Paper
- Pen

Preparation

You will need to "stack the deck" before you perform the trick in a way so that the third card in the deck is a particular one and write the card's name on a piece of paper, place it in the envelope and seal it before putting the envelope in your pocket.

Steps

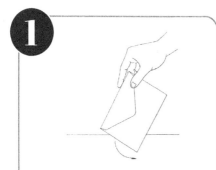

1

Tell your audience that you have made a prediction about which card your volunteer is about to choose; then take the envelope that you have prepared beforehand out of your pocket and put it on the table-you will not be touching it again.

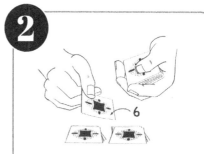

2

Give the deck of cards a quick "false shuffle" and hand them over to the volunteer; ask them to deal out the top six cards into two rows of three cards each. The Card should be in the top row on the right-hand side.

3

Ask the volunteer to point to a row.

a) If they point to the top row, remove the bottom row.

b) If they choose the bottom row, also take away the bottom row.

Pretend that their choice is what helped you decide on which row to move away.

4

Ask the volunteer to pick two cards, if they pick the first two cards, take away those and the remaining card is their card and move onto step seven.

5

a) If the volunteer points to the first and third cards, take away the second one and move onto b.

b) Have them point to another card, whichever one they pick, always remove the first card and give them the one on the right, then go to step seven.

6

a) If the volunteer points to the second two cards, take away the first card and go to part b.

b) Ask them to pick another card; whichever one they pick, always remove the first card and give them the right-hand card and go to step seven.

7

Have the volunteer turn over the card you gave to them, then hand over the envelope which will reveal your prediction!

The Lift

Skills Required

- Double Lift
- Sleight of Hand

Steps

1

Straighten up the deck and do the double lift and show the second card to the audience so that they will think it is the top card; then put the cards back on top of the deck.

2

Next take the very top card and place it at the bottom of the deck and the audience should be thinking that you are moving the card that you showed them.

3

Straighten up the deck and tell the audience that you are going to make the bottom card be on top of the pack; perform an action over the top of the deck such as waving a hand or something similar.

4

Now you turn over the top card and it will look like the card jumped from the bottom to the top of the deck!

The Magic Shoe

Skills Needed

- Card Peeking
- False Shuffling
- Sleight of Hand

Props Required

- Handkerchief
- Paper
- Pen
- Shoe

Preparation

Before you gather your audience, look at the top card on the deck, write the name on the piece of paper and put it into your shoe, the handkerchief goes in your pocket.

Steps

Do a fast false shuffle that keeps the top card where it is, then hold the deck in your right hand just above the table and put the handkerchief over the deck of cards.

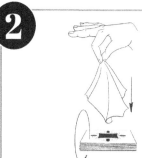

As you're putting the handkerchief over your hand, use your fingers and thumb to turn the deck face up, but it has to be quick so the audience doesn't see.

3

Have a volunteer cut the deck through the handkerchief and put their pile on the table while still covered.

4

Quickly turn the deck back over so it is face down again, with the top card being the same one you peeked at before and use your other hand to move your volunteer's pile so they can't look at it.

5

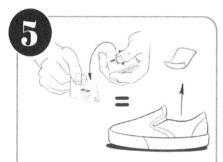

Hand over the pile in your hand to the volunteer and ask them to flip over the top card and say what it is, as they are doing this, take off the shoe that has the paper.

6

Have the volunteer remove the paper and read your prediction.

The Twenty-One Card Trick (Advanced)

Skills Needed

- Memory
- Spelling
- Stacking the Deck (somewhat and optional)

Preparation

*See the basic trick in the previous chapter.

Steps

1

Do steps one to six of the basic version (see previous chapter), but do not reveal the volunteer's card yet. Instead of counting out the eleven cards, you are going to make the reveal a little longer.

2

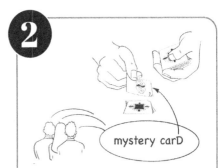

mystery carD

Have your audience spell out "mystery card" and put a card face down for each letter, the card put down with "d" will be the volunteer's card! You also have the option of using a ten letter phrase and flipping over the card after that last letter.

3

There's yet another alternative ending to this trick! Deal the cards into seven face down piles with the card still being the eleventh card that you lay down. Have the volunteer pick four piles, if one has their card, take away the three that don't, otherwise take away the ones they picked.

4

Keep asking the volunteer for piles to take away until you're left with a pile of three cards, then spread them out and announce which is the card.

Conclusion

And now my fellow magicians we have come to the end of our time together. I enjoyed my time with you and am happy knowing that you will soon be moving onto more advanced tricks; just remember that a good magician never reveals their secrets...unless they write a book about it!

Now that you have everything you need to amaze your friends with card tricks, it's time to pass on your newfound knowledge and show other readers where they can find the same help.

Simply by leaving your honest opinion of this book on Amazon, you'll show other beginners where they can find the information they're looking for, and pass their passion for card tricks forward.

Thank you for your help. The joy of magic is kept alive when we pass on our knowledge and you're helping me to do just that! I appreciate you

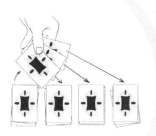

Scan the QR code to leave your review

References

5 Easy Card Tricks You Can Do Today. (n.d.). Www.vanishingincmagic.com. Retrieved September 26, 2021, from https://www.vanishingincmagic.com/learn-card-tricks/five-easy-card-tricks/

False Shuffles - How To Do Them Brief Tutorial. (n.d.). Card-Trick.com. Retrieved September 24, 2021, from https://www.card-trick.com/card-sleights-overview/false-shuffles/

Forcing Cards - A Great Sleight Of Hand Technique. (n.d.). Card-Trick.com. Retrieved September 25, 2021, from https://www.card-trick.com/card-sleights-overview/forcing-cards/

Fullman, J. (2009). Card tricks. Qeb Pub.

History of Card Tricks. (n.d.). Www.vanishingincmagic.com. Retrieved September 27, 2021, from https://www.vanishingincmagic.com/learn-card-tricks/history-of-card-tricks/

How to Do a 21 Card Card Trick. (2021, August 17). WikiHow. https://www.wikihow.com/Do-a-21-Card-Card-Trick

How to Do a Back Palm Vanish. (2021, July 1). WikiHow. https://www.wikihow.com/Do-a-Back-Palm-Vanish

How to Do Easy Card Tricks. (2021, July 1). WikiHow. https://www.wikihow.com/Do-Easy-Card-Tricks

Kawamoto, W. (2019, November 12). 16 Cool Card Tricks for Beginners and Kids. The Spruce Crafts. https://www.thesprucecrafts.com/magic-card-tricks-for-beginners-2267073

Kawamoto, W. (2020a, April 1). Find a Card Easy Magic Trick for Beginners. The Spruce Crafts. https://www.thesprucecrafts.com/best-card-trick-2267052

Kawamoto, W. (2020b, May 13). Learn How to Cut to the Four Aces. The Spruce Crafts. https://www.thesprucecrafts.com/cut-to-four-aces-magic-card-trick-2266982

Lord, E. (2014, December 23). 13 Card Tricks That'll Make You Look Like a Wizard. Bustle. https://www.bustle.com/life/55300-9-easy-card-tricks-that-will-make-you-look-like-basically-a-wizard-video

Mismag822 - The Card Trick Teacher. (2014a, April 10). Easiest

Card Trick Ever. Www.youtube.com. https://www.youtube.com/watch?v=jzjhcfVvWRA&list=WL&index=13

Mismag822 - The Card Trick Teacher. (2014b, May 26). ANYBODY CAN DO THIS Card Trick. Www.youtube.com. https://www.youtube.com/watch?v=xcKlY_D2PRo

Peeking At A Card - How To Perform This Popular Card Sleight. (n.d.). Card-Trick.com. Retrieved September 21, 2021, from https://www.card-trick.com/card-sleights-overview/peeking/

Roya, W. (2019, July 9). How to Get Started in Card Magic. PlayingCardDecks.com. https://playingcarddecks.com/blogs/all-in/how-to-get-started-in-card-magic

Royal Confidante - How This Sleight Of Hand Card Trick Is Done. (n.d.). Card-Trick.com. Retrieved September 28, 2021, from https://www.card-trick.com/card-tricks-using-sleight-of-hand/royal-confidante/

Stop When U Like. (n.d.). Card-Trick.com. Retrieved October 2, 2021, from https://www.card-trick.com/card-tricks-using-sleight-of-hand/stop-when-u-like/

Taylor, C. (2019, January 26). The Features of a Standard Deck of Cards. ThoughtCo. https://www.thoughtco.com/standard-deck-of-cards-3126599

The Double Lift Sleight Of Hand Card Trick: How It's Done. (n.d.). Card-Trick.com. Retrieved September 27, 2021, from https://www.card-trick.com/card-sleights-overview/double-lift/

The False Cut - A Useful Card Sleight In The Repertoire Of Card Magic. (n.d.). Card-Trick.com. Retrieved September 21, 2021, from https://www.card-trick.com/card-sleights-overview/the-false-cut/

The Magic Spell Sleight Of Hand Card Trick - Learn How It's Done. (n.d.). Card-Trick.com. Retrieved September 28, 2021, from https://www.card-trick.com/card-tricks-using-sleight-of-hand/magic-spell/

wikiHow. (2021, September 15). How to Count Cards. WikiHow. https://www.wikihow.com/Count-Cards

Zenon, P. (2008). Simple sleight-of-hand : card and coin tricks for the beginning magician. Rosen Central.

Made in the USA
Las Vegas, NV
15 December 2024